THE WESTHILL PROJECT R.E. 5–16

JEWS

1

Maureen Austerberry

Series editors
JOHN RUDGE
GARTH READ
GEOFF TEECE

Jewish consultants
The Centre for the Study of Judaism
and Jewish Christian Relations

Stanley Thornes (Publishers) Ltd

First published in 1990 by:
Stanley Thornes (Publishers) Ltd
Old Station Drive
Leckhampton
CHELTENHAM GL53 0DN
England

British Library Cataloguing in Publication Data
Austerberry, Maureen
    Jews.
    1, pupils' bk.
    1. Judaism
    I. Title   II. Series
    296

ISBN 1–871402–18–2

Typeset by Kalligraphic Design Ltd, Horley, Surrey
Printed and bound in Hong Kong

Contents

Acknowledgements

The author and publishers are grateful to the following for permission to reproduce copyright material:

Photographs

Cover:
Jerry Wooldridge

Inside pages:
Jerry Wooldridge pages 8, 9, 10, 11, 12, 13, 18 (top), 20, 21 (left), 22, 25, 26, 27, 30, 31, 32, 33, 34, 35, 37, 38, 39, 41, 42, 49, 50, 51, 52 (bottom), 53, 55, 56, 57, 58, 60, 61. Juliette Soester pages 18 (bottom), 21 (right), 52 (top).

The illustrations on pages 5, 6, 7, 14, 15, 16, 17, 23, 24, 28, 29, 32, 36 and 40 are by Alice Englander. Those on pages 43, 44, 45, 46, 47, 48, 54 and 59 are by Edward Ripley.

1 Jewish community life

People

We all need other people.
Babies need grown-ups to care
for them.

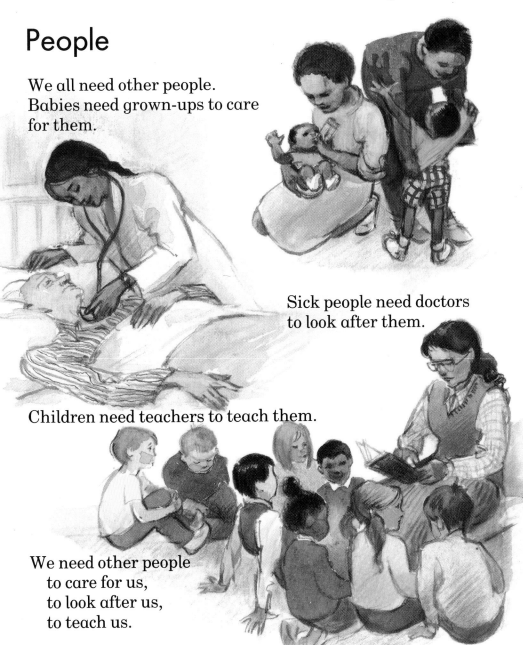

Sick people need doctors
to look after them.

Children need teachers to teach them.

We need other people
  to care for us,
  to look after us,
  to teach us.

In your street you may find
 people who care for others,
 people who look after others,
 people who teach others.

People who live near each other and do things for each other are a community. Your school is a community. Your neighbourhood is a community. The people in a community need each other.

People in a community are not all the same. Some have round faces and others thin faces. There are people with green eyes and people with blue or brown eyes. Some people have fair hair and others black hair. Hair can be curly or straight.

Can you think of some things that make people different?

People are different from each other, but people who are different can belong together and need each other. People who are different can belong to the same community.

Jews

Many people belong to Jewish communities, but all Jews are not the same.

Many Jewish people believe in God. They have some special books about God and the most important of these is called the Torah.

Jewish people have a special day each week which is set aside for rest. It is called Shabbat.

Lots of different people belong to Jewish communities. When they meet together they all worship God and study the Torah.

Places where Jews meet

Jewish communities have special places where they meet. These places are called synagogues. All synagogues do not look the same. Here are pictures of different synagogues.

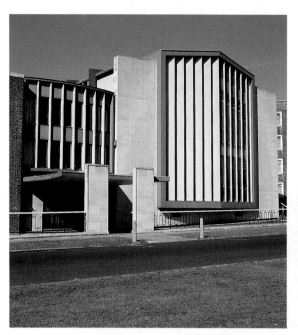

This is a picture of the inside of a synagogue. It shows the main big room of the synagogue. This room has lots of seats. There is a downstairs part and an upstairs gallery. In this synagogue men sit downstairs while women sit upstairs in the gallery.

This synagogue is very different from home or school or shops. It is a place of worship.

When the people who belong to the Jewish community meet with their friends at this synagogue they read and study the Torah and they pray to God.

In the synagogue there are things which remind Jewish people of God. On one wall there is a cupboard with a curtain in front of it. This cupboard is called the ark. Near the ark there is a lamp which never goes out. It reminds Jews that they believe that God is always present.

The copy of the Torah in the synagogue is handwritten on a scroll and is kept inside the ark.

In the middle of the synagogue there is a raised platform. This is the bimah. On the bimah there is a desk where the Torah is rolled out ready for reading. When they hear the Torah and pray, the Jewish people are worshipping God.

This is a picture of the inside of another synagogue. In this synagogue the people all sit together. See if you can find the ark, the bimah and the Torah.

Christopher visits a synagogue

David was pleased it was Saturday morning. Mummy said that Christopher from next door could come with them to the morning service at their synagogue. Christopher was waiting at his gate when the Cohens walked down their path. Mrs Cohen was holding Rachel's hand.

'Hi, Christopher. Have you got a cap to wear?' said Mr Cohen. Christopher shook his head.

'Never mind,' said Mr Cohen. 'There are spare ones at the synagogue. All the men and boys have to wear a cap or hat inside the synagogue.'

They walked along a number of streets before they reached the synagogue. Christopher followed the Cohens into the hallway where everyone was talking and greeting friends.

Mrs Cohen said, 'Rachel and I are going to sit with the ladies in the gallery. David, look after Christopher – he's a guest.'

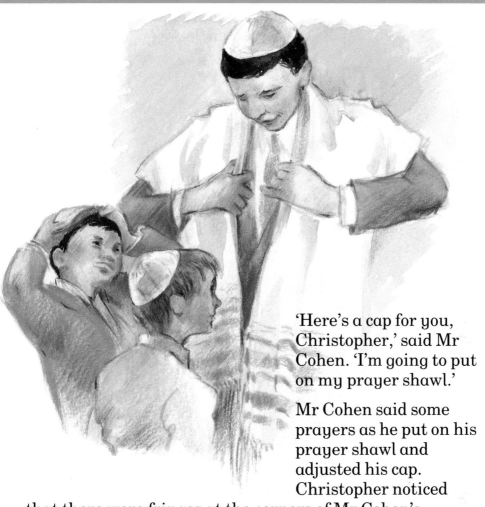

'Here's a cap for you, Christopher,' said Mr Cohen. 'I'm going to put on my prayer shawl.'

Mr Cohen said some prayers as he put on his prayer shawl and adjusted his cap. Christopher noticed that there were fringes at the corners of Mr Cohen's prayer shawl. The boys put on their caps and followed Mr Cohen into the main room. They sat together.

'Look, Christopher – there's Mummy and Rachel sitting in the gallery,' said David. Rachel gave them a little wave.

The service had already started. Christopher noticed a man standing on a platform. Sometimes he sang alone and sometimes all the people sang with him.

Christopher whispered to Mr Cohen, 'I don't understand the words.' Mr Cohen said, 'The service is in a language called Hebrew. Look.' He opened his service book and showed Christopher the Hebrew writing on one side and English on the other.

David whispered to Christopher, 'I'm glad we haven't missed the best bit of the service when they open the ark and take out the scroll of the Torah.'

Everyone stood up when this began. Two men opened the doors of the ark and another took out the scroll of the Torah and carried it carefully to the table on the platform. David nudged Christopher when Mr Cohen was called up to read the Torah. After the readings, the scroll of the Torah was again carefully put back into the ark.

'Who is that?' asked Christopher, pointing to a man dressed in a black gown.

'That's the rabbi,' said David. 'He is going to talk to us about the readings.' The rabbi then talked in English about the readings from the Torah. There were more prayers and singing before the service finished. Afterwards everyone went into another room where tables were set out with little glasses of wine and plates of biscuits. The room became full of noisy, laughing people. People were joking and shaking hands. Then the rabbi clapped his hands and everyone was quiet. He said a prayer and the people had a little wine and something to eat. Mr and Mrs Cohen talked with their friends. David and Christopher ate their biscuits and sipped the wine.

Soon it was time to go home. When they came to Christopher's gate everyone said goodbye. Christopher rushed in to tell his Mummy all about his visit to the synagogue.

At the synagogue

Christopher learnt a lot of new things when he went to the synagogue with David. He learnt about some of the people who took part in the worship.

Leaders

There are two special people who help in the worship at the synagogue, the rabbi and the hazzan.

A rabbi is a teacher. Rabbis are trained to teach the Torah to the people. They are usually responsible for the worship in the synagogue and they may preach a sermon explaining parts of the Torah. The rabbis often have special seats in the synagogue. Usually they are present at various ceremonies. Some wear black gowns, others their ordinary clothes.

The hazzan leads the singing in the synagogue. This is usually done without the help of musical instruments. The hazzan often has a very beautiful voice. A hazzan stands on the bimah in front of the reading desk, facing the ark. Sometimes there is a choir to help with the singing of songs and prayers.

The Hebrew language

During the service Christopher did not understand most of the words. Do you remember why?

In many synagogues all the service is in the Hebrew language. In others, parts of the service are in the local language. Hebrew is a very old language and is the language in which the Torah is written. It is read from right to left. When you write anything, in which direction do your words go?

Here are some Hebrew words.

In English these words mean, 'Blessed are you, Lord our God, King of the universe.' Many Jewish prayers start with these words.

Worship in the synagogue

Jews worship God by praying, by singing, and by reading the Torah.

Praying and singing

Jewish people believe that they can talk to God and listen to God. Talking with God is called praying.

In the synagogue sometimes a hazzan says or chants the prayers alone. Sometimes everyone joins in the prayers with the hazzan.

Prayers can be said sitting or standing.

Some people find rocking backwards and forwards helps them to pray. Sometimes Jewish men pull their prayer shawl over their head to help them forget about other things and to think about God.

Sometimes Jews sing songs and verses of the Torah when they worship God. There are songs for special occasions. Some are slow and sad and others are quick and cheerful.

Rituals

Rituals are special things that people do over and over again. Jews do many special things when they worship and some of these they do over and over again. These are rituals which help them to worship God.

Reading the Torah

During Christopher's visit to the synagogue he and David watched as the scrolls of the Torah were taken out of the ark and read from the bimah. For most Jews, reading the Torah in the synagogue is an important ritual. It begins with opening the ark. Two people hold the doors open, while another carefully carries the scroll. Sometimes it is taken round parts of the synagogue. While the scroll is being carried round the synagogue many people touch the scroll with the fringe of their prayer shawl – others may bow as the scroll is carried past them. They do this to show that the Torah is very precious to them. Another person helps to take off the beautiful covering from the scroll. It is then unrolled, ready for reading.

The person who reads the Torah uses a special pointer instead of a finger to follow the writing. This also shows that the Torah is very precious and important.

Jewish people feel that it is a great honour to read the Torah during a service in the synagogue.

Kiddush

Do you remember that after the service Christopher enjoyed having some wine and biscuits? This took place in a different room from the one where the service was held. This ritual is called Kiddush.

During this ritual some special prayers are said or sung over a cup of wine. These prayers are a blessing for Shabbat, the Jewish day of rest.

Glasses of wine are passed around for all to enjoy. Sometimes there are cakes or biscuits to eat. Many people use this time to talk to friends and newcomers. This happy ritual helps each person to feel a part of the Jewish community.

Helping other people

In every community there are people who need help. Perhaps a next-door neighbour needs help with shopping, or a parent needs a babysitter. Did you need someone to help you today?

In every community there are people who help others.

Did you help someone today? A friend? An old person? A little brother or sister?

It is not always easy to help other people. You have to give up some of your time. You may have to share some of your money. You may have to work very hard to help other people.

Jews helping other people

Jews believe that God wants people to help each other. Jews try to obey and please God. Here are some words from the Torah which tell Jews to help other people.

וְאָהַבְתָּ לְרֵעֲךָ כָּמוֹךָ

These words are written in Hebrew. In English they mean, 'Love other people as yourself.'

Jews try to care for other people.

They may give money to help poor people.

Jews may care for old people.

They may care for young people.

Jews may care for the sick. There are many Jewish doctors and nurses.

Jews may show their love and care for children by teaching them in Jewish schools.

They do all these things because they believe that God cares for people everywhere. If they are to show their love of God, they too must care for people.

2 Jewish family life

Homes

Most people spend a lot of time at home. Homes are places
where people live and where they feel they belong.
All homes are not the same.

Some homes are very big
with large gardens.

Some homes are small with
no garden at all, and some
homes are in tall blocks of
flats.

Some people say that it does not matter how big or small your
home is. It is what you have in your home and what you do
in your home that is important.

Things people have in their homes

'We have a ramp in our home for my Mum's wheelchair.'

'In the front room I keep photos of all my family.'

'Upstairs in our house we have a play room where we can do anything we like. I've got lots and lots of Lego. Sometimes my sister plays school. Once she chalked on the wallpaper and then she got into trouble!'

'We have a cupboard full of the best china. We get it out for special parties. I have to help wash it. I have to be careful not to drop any of it, or Mum and Dad will be very cross with me!'

Things people do in their homes

'We leave our shoes in the back kitchen and go round the house in socks or slippers.'

'We have a rule in our home that the TV goes off when visitors call. It always happens when it is my favourite programme. I hate it.'

'Grandma always comes to our house for Sunday dinner.'

'On your birthday you don't do any work, not even washing up.'

'We don't eat meat in our home.'

Jewish homes

Mezuzah

Jewish families have many things and follow customs in their homes to remind them of their religion.

Most Jews have very small copies of part of the Torah on the doorposts in their homes. These words are handwritten on a very small scroll and placed inside a little box or tube. The box with its scroll inside is called a mezuzah.

The words on the scroll in the mezuzah are part of a prayer called the Shema. The Shema is a prayer that begins, 'Hear O Israel, the Lord is our God, the Lord is one.'

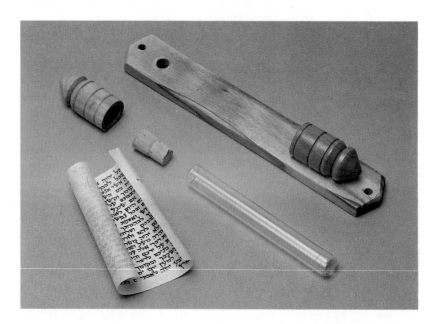

Many Jews touch the mezuzah with their fingers when they go through the doorway. Doing this helps them to show their love and respect for God and God's laws.

A Jewish kitchen

Can you see anything unusual in this kitchen? Some of the things you can see show that it is a Jewish kitchen.

This family has just been to the shops. Some of the packets they have bought have Hebrew words on them. This shows that they are foods which have been prepared for Jewish people.

Jewish people have a rule that they must not mix food with meat in it with food with milk in it. So one set of saucepans is kept for meat and one set for milk. They wash them up in different sinks or bowls. They also use two sets of knives and forks, one for each kind of food.

Some families have a poster on the wall to remind them of the different prayers they say when they eat their food.

Rules about food

Jewish families have rules about how to prepare food and rules about foods they are allowed to eat and those they are not allowed to eat. These rules are written in the Torah. They believe that these rules have come from God.

One of the packets of food on the kitchen table in the picture has the Hebrew word כשר on it. This word 'kasher' is used by Jews to describe those foods that they are allowed to eat and that have been prepared in the Jewish way.

Here are some foods that Jewish people are not allowed to eat at any time.

Meal blessings

Having meals together is an important part of Jewish family life. Many Jewish people think it is important to recite blessings or short prayers before they eat their food. The father or mother says a blessing at the beginning of the meal, thanking God for food.

This blessing is said over the bread.

בָּרוּךְ אַתָּה יְיָ אֱלֹהֵינוּ מֶלֶךְ הָעוֹלָם ·
הַמּוֹצִיא לֶחֶם מִן הָאָרֶץ :

In English this means, 'Blessed are you, O Lord our God, King of the universe, who brings forth bread from the earth.'

The girl in the picture is going to eat an apple. Here is the blessing she is learning to say when she eats apples: 'Blessed are you, O Lord our God, King of the universe, who creates the fruit of the tree.'

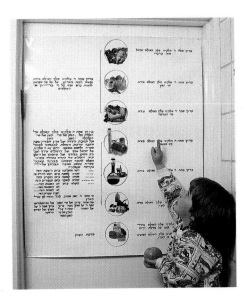

Praying at home

Many Jewish men say morning prayers before having their breakfast. Most Jewish women find time for their prayers during the course of the day.

This man is getting ready for morning prayers at home. First he covers his head with a small cap called a kippah. Some Jews wear this cap all the time as a sign of respect for God. Next he puts on his prayer shawl or tallit.

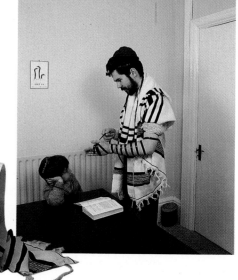

Then he takes up the tefillin, two little boxes containing words from the Torah, and ties one on his left arm and the other around his head with the straps.

As he does all these actions, he has special prayers to say. Then he says morning prayers using the Jewish prayer book. These prayers always include the Shema. Do you remember the first words of the Shema? Perhaps you could look back in this book and find the opening words.

When this man wears these clothes and says these prayers at the beginning of each day he remembers how important it is for him to follow the Jewish way of life for the rest of the day.

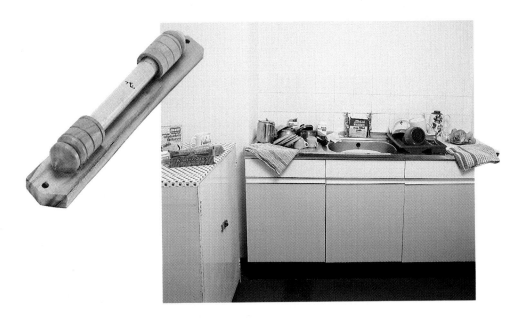

Jewish people think that their homes are important places in which to worship God and keep God's laws. Some of the things they have in their homes and many of the things they do together there, help them follow the Jewish way of life and show they belong to the Jewish community.

Celebrating special days

Many families celebrate some important days each year.

When we celebrate we often have extra nice food and perhaps wear our best clothes. Sometimes we decorate our homes and, if other people are joining in the celebration, we may visit each other's homes.

Does your family celebrate some important days each year?

What do you celebrate at these times?

How does your family make the day special?

Jewish families celebrating

Jews have many special times in the year to celebrate. Many families look forward to these times each year. Sometimes they have ceremonies or special food to eat on these days.

Do you know the names of some Jewish celebrations? Let's learn about four of them.

One is called Shabbat.

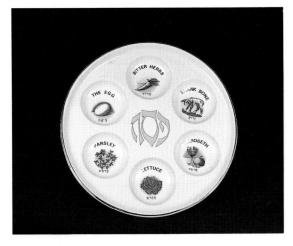

Another is called Pesah.

Another is called Sukkot.

The fourth one is called Hanukkah.

Shabbat

Friday evening is a special time for Jews. It is the beginning of the weekly celebrations of Shabbat. Shabbat starts on Friday evening and ends on Saturday evening. It is a day of rest and worship.

Jews believe that God has told them to keep the day holy by using it for rest and for worship. Many Jews make sure that they do not do any work at all on this day.

Just before it is dark on Friday night, the family gather round a table. When everybody is ready the mother lights two candles. She shades her eyes from the light. Everyone round the table is quiet and the candlelight flickers. Then she says the blessing to welcome Shabbat.

After this short ceremony, some Jews go to the synagogue to join with others in welcoming Shabbat.

When they return home the Shabbat celebrations continue. Again the family gathers round the table. Fathers and mothers bless each of their children, and everyone wishes each other a peaceful Shabbat, using the Hebrew words, 'Shabbat shalom'.

One of the older members of the family, usually the father, holds a cup of wine and says the blessing for the wine and the Shabbat. Everyone says 'Amen', which means 'So be it'. While they are standing they have a little drink of wine. After everyone is seated, the father lifts up the special loaves of bread which are specially baked for Shabbat. He then says a blessing, breaks the bread and gives everyone a piece.

Then the family have their evening meal. Some families enjoy singing Jewish songs to help make the evening of Shabbat a happy one.

For most Jews the rest of Shabbat until sunset on Saturday is a time to relax and enjoy being together as a family.

Some do not do any work at all on this day. Some do not travel very far during Shabbat. Some like to go for a walk or play in the park. Others like to read quietly at home.

These people want Shabbat to be different from all the other days of the week.

For some families the end of the Shabbat on Saturday evening is also marked by special rituals. This time the father fills the cup to overflowing with wine. One of the children may hold a twisted candle. There is a box of sweet-smelling spice on the table. After some blessings are recited, the spice box is passed round for everyone to smell. At the end of the ritual the candle is put out by dipping it in some wine. When the light goes out, Shabbat is over and a new week has begun.

They all then say to each other in Hebrew, 'Shavua tov', which in English means 'Have a good week'.

During the week, many Jewish families like to remember how they enjoyed their Shabbat together. They also look forward to how they are going to spend the next Shabbat.

The festival of Pesah

Getting ready for Pesah

Every spring, Jewish families get ready to celebrate Pesah. Pesah is the festival that is sometimes called Passover.

It is important that the house is really clean before the festival begins. Some families get rid of all things made with flour, like biscuits, spaghetti and bread. The children sometimes enjoy helping their mother to look for things that must be thrown out. They clean the cupboards and burn any rubbish.

As well as cleaning the house and seeing that all food made with flour is removed, Jewish families get out special dishes and cutlery that they use only during these celebrations.

All this busy preparation reminds Jews how important this festival is. It is a time, each year, when they remember a very old story which is part of their Torah. It is a story about a great escape that happened many thousands of years ago.

The great escape

The slaves crying in Egypt

Long ago when the Jews lived in Egypt, the king of Egypt,
or pharaoh, treated them as slaves. He made them build
big cities. They had to work all day long in the hot sun and
to carry heavy loads. Their hands were sore and their legs
were tired. Sometimes the cruel master whipped them.
The slaves cried and cried. Sometimes they were too tired
even to cry.

They longed to be free. Free from such hard work; free
from harsh men shouting at them; free to do what they
wanted to do. Some Jews cried to God to save them from
their cruel slave-masters.

A slave's baby is saved

One day the pharaoh's daughter was bathing in the river when she saw a little Jewish baby floating in a basket among the reeds. She knew that her father had said that Jewish baby boys were to be killed. She realised that this baby's mother must be trying to save the baby's life. The princess was so moved by the mother's bravery, love and care that she took the baby back to her home. She called the baby Moses, which means 'taken from the water'.

The princess cared for Moses as though he was her own son. However, even though Moses grew up in the palace, surrounded by luxury, he never forgot that he was really a Jewish slave and not an Egyptian prince.

God hears the cries of the slaves

God heard the cries of the Jewish slaves and many years later God sent Moses to be their leader. Moses with his brother Aaron went to the court of Pharaoh and asked, 'O most noble king, we your humble slaves ask that we might be allowed to go into the desert and worship our God.'

The pharaoh said, 'No. Go back to your work.'

Again and again Moses went and pleaded with the pharaoh to let the Jews go free. Each time the pharaoh refused. And each time God sent a plague on the land. Frogs came up out of the Nile and swarmed everywhere. Dust turned to maggots, dense swarms of flies flew everywhere. The cattle fell ill and people suffered from nasty boils. Still Pharaoh refused to let the Jews go. God sent further plagues. One day there was an enormous thunderstorm with hailstones as large as a man's fist. The next plague was a storm of locusts, which ate up every green leaf and blade of grass. Then there was a plague of darkness when people could not see one another for three whole days.

The awful night

Moses might have given up hope by this time. But he believed that God had told him to go again to Pharaoh and ask him to let the slaves go.

'No, that is my last word,' said the pharaoh.

Then Moses told him about the last and most awful plague that would happen. 'O mighty Pharaoh, God has said that if you will not let my people go then every first-born person and animal will die.'

However, God had made a plan to save the slaves from this awful plague. Moses told the slaves to smear their doorpost with the blood of a lamb so that the angel of death would know to pass over that household and they would be safe.

On that awful night many animals died. Many people died. Even Pharaoh's first-born son became sick and died. People were sad and afraid at the terrible things that were happening. Nobody in the slaves' families died because their houses were marked with blood on the doorposts.

The slaves get ready to go

The Egyptians were so frightened that they begged the slaves to leave their country straight away. So the slaves decided that they must go as quickly as possible, before the Egyptians changed their minds. They packed their belongings. They gathered their animals together. Food for the journey was prepared. Because there was no time to make bread with yeast and wait for it to rise, they made some flat bread instead. Before they left they had a hurried meal. It would help them to keep going until they were out of the reach of Pharaoh and his soldiers.

God guided the Jewish slaves along the way. They travelled by night and by day. They were anxious to be out of Egypt as soon as possible.

They were near the Red Sea when Pharaoh and his army could be seen in the distance. Pharaoh had changed his mind and wanted to have his slaves back again. Everyone was afraid. They would be caught by Pharaoh or drowned in the Red Sea.

The escape to freedom

Then God told Moses what to do. Moses stretched out his hand over the sea, and God drove the sea away all night with a strong east wind and turned the sea-bed into dry land. The waters were torn apart, and the Jews went through the sea on dry ground, while the waters made a wall for them to the right and to the left.

Pharaoh, his chariots and his cavalry chased after the Jews, but they got stuck in the mud. The seas came thundering in and drowned Pharaoh and all his army.

The Jews were free at last. Their hearts were full of thankfulness and praise for God. They believed that God had saved them from drowning and set them free from the Egyptians, so they all joined together in singing songs in praise of God.

Pesah begins

The festival of Pesah, or Passover, reminds Jewish families of the story of the slaves' escape to freedom.

On the first night of the festival, Jewish families have a special meal. It is called the Seder. Sometimes they invite other relatives and friends to celebrate this meal with them. All the guests wear their best clothes. The supper table is set very carefully with all the special things that help to make this a celebration meal.

What do you see on the table?

Did you notice the books on the table? These are copies of a book called the Hagaddah and it contains the story of how the Jews escaped from slavery in Egypt. This story is used during the Seder meal.

The Seder meal

In the middle of the table there is an unusual plate called
the Seder plate.

In the middle of this plate there is a bowl of salty water.
Round the outside there are small dishes of different foods.
When the father of the family reads the story from the
Hagaddah he uses these things to help the family
remember the important parts of the story.

Here are some foods on the Seder plate which are used by the father to remind the family of the sad parts of the story.

The food on the plate in this picture is called haroset. It is made of chopped nuts, apples and cinnamon mixed together with wine. When the family eat this mixture they remember the mortar with which the slaves had to make bricks. The bricks were used to build many of the large buildings in which the Egyptians lived.

On another dish on the Seder plate there are some herbs. When people eat these they taste very bitter. The family eat some of these during the Seder meal to remind them of how the slaves were hurt by the cruel slave-masters.

What foods have you tried that tasted bitter or sweet to you?

Are there any foods which you eat at special times in the year?

Have you ever tasted your own tears when you cried? Did you notice that they were salty? Jewish families have salty water during the Seder meal to remind them that many slaves often cried during their time in Egypt. The slaves cried because of the cruel ways in which their masters treated them when they were making bricks and building houses. The slaves also cried when they longed for a time when they would be free.

Here are some more of the things that Jewish families do during the Seder meal to help them remember other parts of the story of the slaves' escape from Egypt.

Do you remember in the story how the Egyptians suffered ten plagues? During the meal everyone round the table calls out the names of each of these plagues. Each time a plague is called out they dip a finger in the cup and let a drop of wine fall onto the saucer. This helps the family to remember that many other people suffered a lot of pain before the Jewish slaves were able to go free.

Do you remember that the slaves had to bake some bread in a hurry on the night before they escaped to freedom? It was made without yeast. Throughout the whole festival of Pesah, Jewish people only eat a bread called matzah to remind them of this part of the story. Matzah bread is flat and crisp and tastes rather like cream crackers. During the Seder meal a game is played with the children. The father tells the children to close their eyes and then he hides a piece of matzah somewhere in the room. Later on the children look for the hidden piece. The one who finds it is given a present. Everybody enjoys eating the piece which is found and the Seder meal is over.

The festival of Sukkot

Jewish families have another important festival each year which is called Sukkot. The word Sukkot means huts. The festival reminds them of the story of the long time the Jewish slaves spent wandering in the desert after their escape from Egypt. During this time they built shelters from the sun, the sand and the wind. At night as the wanderers lay in these temporary shelters they often looked at the distant moon and stars. They thought how great it was to be free. Many of them felt they wanted to thank God for setting them free and giving them enough food and shelter to survive in the desert.

Getting ready for Sukkot

This is an exciting time for most Jewish families. They build a hut or booth in their garden. This hut is called a sukkah. All kinds of materials are needed. The family collect pieces of wood for the walls and evergreen branches to put on the roof. They try to make sure that they can see the open sky through the branches on the roof. They all have a lot of fun decorating their huts with fresh fruit, flowers and pictures that the children may have painted. They may also put tables and chairs and even beds in their huts.

Celebrating Sukkot

Shabbat

Shabbat is an important day each week for Jewish people. During the festival of Sukkot the ceremonies to welcome Shabbat are done in the family sukkah.

Eating

Families make sure that they eat at least one meal a day in their huts. This reminds them that it is a time when they thank God for food and shelter.

Visiting

During the festival, families visit each other and enjoy eating together in each other's huts. The children often enjoy seeing whose hut is the best.

Sleeping

Many Jewish people, especially those who live in warm countries, enjoy sleeping out in their booths during the eight days of the festival. They will be able to look up at the stars as the wandering Jews did many years ago. Of course they do not sleep out if it is raining.

The festival of Sukkot is also a harvest festival. It is a time when Jewish people celebrate and give thanks for the harvesting of crops.

All people need food. Without food we will become weak, sick, and die.

Many people like to say 'thank you' for food and for the ways in which the earth produces it. During the festival of Sukkot Jewish people are thanking God for food.

Do you ever feel thankful for all the good things you have to eat?

Lights are very important to us all.

Lights help us to see. They may warn us of danger. They make things bright and happy.

The festival of Hanukkah

Another important festival for Jewish families is called Hanukkah. This festival also reminds Jewish people of a very old story. The story is about the lighting of a lamp.

Long ago in Israel, Jews worshipped God in the Temple at Jerusalem. It was a beautiful place. One day foreign soldiers captured it and spoilt it. They knocked down the big lamp in the centre of the Temple which reminded Jewish people of God. When they did this, the oil in the lamp ran everywhere. The soldiers also made sacrifices to idols which they had brought into the Temple.

After a time a very famous Jewish person called Judas Maccabaeus and his soldiers fought a hard battle with the enemy and regained the Temple for the Jews.

Before the Temple could be used again for worship it had to be cleaned. The lamp of God that was always burning in the Temple had to have special oil. Without this special oil the lamp would not burn. They could find only one pot of this oil. It should have been enough to last for only one day. The Jewish people were very surprised when they found that the lamp kept burning for eight days, without needing any more oil. Many of the Jews said it was a miracle which God had done for them.

The festival of Hanukkah in the home

Hanukkah, or the festival of lights, lasts for eight days.

On each day a candle is lit and set in a special candle holder called a hanukkiah. On the first day one candle is lit. On the second day two are lit, and so on until all eight are lit. In fact there are nine candles, one being used to light the others. This candle is called the servant.

Perhaps you can tell your friends why there are eight candles to light on the holder.

Hanukkah is a time for celebration and parties. Many children enjoy eating the special cakes that are made for this festival. These cakes are called latkes. Children are given presents. A favourite game played by Jewish children at these parties is called spinning the dreidel. This dreidel has four sides and on each side there is a Hebrew letter.

Hanukkah is a festival of lights. During the festival Jewish people are remembering the way in which the lamp of God was kept alight in a strange and mysterious way in the Temple at Jerusalem.

Notes for teachers

This book is the first in the Westhill Project's series of four books about Jews. It is designed for children of 7 to 9 years old in the lower junior school. Jewish practices and beliefs are described clearly and without any assumptions being made about any teacher's or pupil's acceptance of the Jewish faith now or in the future.

Depending on their abilities, some children will be able to read parts of the book for themselves, while others may need more help, or benefit from having parts read to them. The stories can be read to groups of all abilities, and the pictures accompanying the text may help younger pupils to follow it. In any case, the method you choose will need to suit both the particular children you are teaching and the scheme of work into which you are introducing the book.

There are two parts to the book. Part One introduces children to some of the important features of Jewish communities. In Part Two they learn about aspects of Jewish family life. The Jewish community is dealt with first so that children have some idea of basic Jewish beliefs and practices before they consider the specifically religious aspects of Jewish family life. The two parts are indicated by colour coding around the page number: pink for Part One and blue for Part Two.

In *Jews 1*, pupils are introduced to several key words and concepts which are considered essential for their continuing religious education.

Human experience words: community, rituals, ceremonies, belonging, needing, sharing, caring, helping, celebrating
General religious words: God, prayer, worship, belief, blessing
Jewish words: Jews, Torah, Shabbat, synagogue, ark, scroll, bimah, rabbi, hazzan, Hebrew, Kiddush, mezuzah, Shema, kasher, kippah, tallit, tefillin, Pesah, Seder, Hagaddah, Sukkot, Hanukkah

Content overview of the pupils' books
The four *Jews* pupils' books are designed to help pupils develop an understanding of Judaism as a world religion. Each book deals with different aspects of Jewish practices, beliefs and experiences.

The diagrammatic presentation below indicates the content of each book and shows how children are helped to build up their knowledge and understanding of this religion in a progressive way from age 7 to 16. The shaded areas in the circles indicate the aspects of Judaism dealt with in particular books.

A more detailed explanation of this is given in the teacher's books, *How do I teach R.E.?* and *Judaism*.

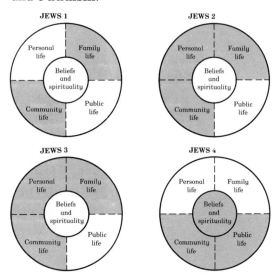

Other materials in this Project
Teachers using this book with junior children should realise that it is only one resource item designed to meet one specific aspect of the primary child's experience of R.E. – learning about Jews, through the words and concepts outlined above. To expand the range of classroom activities designed to meet this need, a **photopack**, with additional pictures and information, is also available.

Teachers using these resources are strongly recommended to refer to the two teacher's books: *How do I teach R.E.?* – the main Project manual and *Judaism* – a source book and guide to the teaching of this religion. A suggested scheme of work is to be found in the latter.

Books and photopacks relating to other religious traditions and various Life Themes are also part of **The Westhill Project R.E. 5–16**.